Turbulent Planet

Shaky Ground

Earthquakes

Mary Colson

Raintree

Chicago, Illinois

For information, address the publisher:
Raintree, 100 N. LaSalle, Suite 1200, Chicago, IL 60602
Printed and bound in China
08 07 06 05 04
10 9 8 7 6 5 4 3 2 1

Library of Congress Cataloging-in-Publication Data
Colson, Mary, 1961-
  Shaky ground / Mary Colson.
      p. cm. -- (Turbulent planet)
Summary: Presents information on earthquakes and their effect
on planetEarth, giving specific examples from around the world.
Includes bibliographical references and index.
  ISBN 1-4109-0589-6 (lib. bdg.), 1-4109-1027-X (Pbk.)
  1. Earthquakes--Juvenile literature. 2. Plate tectonics--Juvenile
literature. 3. Earth--Internal structure--Juvenile literature. [1.
Earthquakes. 2. Plate tectonics. 3. Earth--Internal structure. 4.
Geology.] I. Title. II. Series: Colson, Mary, 1961- Turbulent planet.
  QE521.3.G39 2004
  551.22--dc21
                        2003008296

Acknowledgments
The publisher would like to thank the following for permission to reproduce photographs:
P. 4 The Art Archive; pp. 4–5, 10–11, 11 Rex Features; pp. 5 (top), 20 NOAA/Associated Press; pp. 5 (middle), 18
(right), 20–21, 28, 28–29, 36 (right) Corbis; pp. 5 (bottom), 17, 18 (left), 21, 26, 27 Bettman/Corbis; p. 8 Sipa
Press/Rex Features; pp. 8–9 David Hosking/FLPA; p. 12 Lloyd Cluff/Corbis; p. 13 David Parker/Science Photo
Library; p. 14 The Regents of the University of California and the National Information Service for Earthquake
Engineering; p. 15 NOAA/National Geophysical Data Center; p. 16 Jet Propulsion Laboratory/NASA; p. 19 Carlos
Munoz-Yague/Science Photo Library; p. 22 ABC Ajansi/Corbis Sygma; pp. 22–23 Peter Turnley/Corbis; p. 23
NASA; pp. 24, 45 Pana-Jiji/PA Photos; pp. 24–25, 29, 34, 34–35, 38–39, 41 EPA/PA Photos; p. 25
Reuters/Popperfoto; pp. 26–27 Popperfoto; p. 30 (left and right) USDA/FLPA; p. 31 (top) Andes Press
Agency/Caretas; p. 31 (bottom) James H. Robinson/Oxford Scientific Films; p. 32 National Information Service for
Earthquake Engineering, University of California at Berkeley; p. 32–33, 36 (left) Roy Garner/Rex Features; p. 33
Massimo Sestini/Rex Features; p. 35 Oswaldo Rivas/Reuters; p. 37 Roger Ressmeyer/Corbis; p. 38 Rex Features; p.
39 The Red Cross; p. 40 (left) Steve Lewis/Andes Press Agency; p. 40 (right) Richard Cummins/Corbis; p. 42 Lonely
Planet Images; pp. 42–43 Getty Images News & Sports; p. 42 Lonely Planet Images; p. 43 PA Photos; p. 44 Rex
Features. Cover photograph reproduced with permission of Tom Wagner/Corbis.

Contents

Some words are shown in bold, **like this.** You can find out what they mean by looking in the glossary. You can also look out for them in the "Wild Words" box at the bottom of each page.

Quiver and Quake

Imagine being **jolted** awake in the middle of the night. Your house is shaking so strongly that you are lifted off your bed into the air. Your heart races. All around you it is pitch black. You do not know what to think. Cupboard doors are banging. What on earth is going on?

You can hear your dresser wobble and books falling off shelves. You try to turn the lamp on, but there is no power. The glass in the window cracks and splinters. You try to get out of the room, but the dresser falls over and blocks your way. And still the ground shakes . . . .

Before Pompeii (in Italy) △
was destroyed by a volcanic
eruption, it was **devastated** by
earthquakes in 62 c.e. and 79 c.e.

buckle   twist or bend out of shape
crevice   narrow crack or opening in the earth or rock

Earth-shattering

Outside, buildings crumble. Roads are split open and railroad tracks **buckle**. Bridges snap and skyscrapers topple. People take shelter wherever they can. The earth continues to shake, and a few seconds feel like a lifetime. Houses fall into **crevices** in the earth and sections of land slide down hills. Telephone poles collapse and the phones are dead.

And just when the shaking stops, the fires start.

Chaos

Gas and water pipes burst and there are fires all over town. The emergency services struggle because thick black smoke makes it hard to see and difficult to breathe. People help to dig out their neighbors. They call out to loved ones to see if they are okay. The fires are getting worse, and people are still in danger.

Find out later...

Do all earthquakes happen on land?

How can an earthquake inland cause waves at sea?

How do people measure earthquakes?

Even modern buildings and bridges cannot stand up to the biggest quakes, such as the one in Kobe, Japan, in 1995. △

devastate   cause great destruction
jolted   shaken suddenly

Collision Course

Why does the ground suddenly start to shake? It is all because of the way the earth is made. Our planet is made up of three main parts. In the very middle, there is an ultrahot center called the **core.** The inner core is solid and the outer core is liquid rock. Around the core, there is the **mantle.** Here, liquid rock and gases mix and boil. On the outside there is the **crust.** This is the layer of rock on which the oceans and land sit.

Cracked shell

The earth's crust is broken up into about 30 pieces, or **plates,** of different sizes. The plates move and press against each other. This can create mountains, **valleys,** seas, and earthquakes. The movement of the plates is called **plate tectonics.**

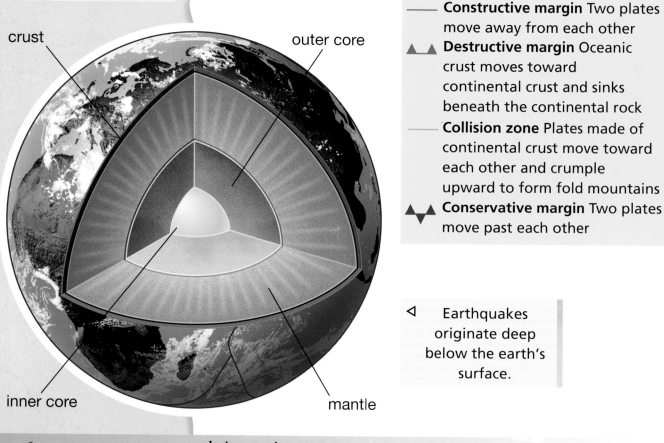

crust

outer core

inner core

mantle

The Earth's Plate Margins ▷
—— **Constructive margin** Two plates move away from each other
▲▲ **Destructive margin** Oceanic crust moves toward continental crust and sinks beneath the continental rock
—— **Collision zone** Plates made of continental crust move toward each other and crumple upward to form fold mountains
▲▼ **Conservative margin** Two plates move past each other

◁ Earthquakes originate deep below the earth's surface.

Wild Words   chain reaction   when one thing causes another to happen
communities   places or towns where people live together

Plate tectonics tells us why there are high **ridges** and deep **trenches** in the oceans. It shows us how mountains and volcanoes are made. It also tells us why the ground beneath our feet is not quite as firm as we think it is.

Chain reaction

When the plates move deep underground, they can set off a chain of events on the surface of the planet. This is called a **chain reaction.** Sometimes these underground movements make a volcano erupt. But this is not the end of the chain— there is more reacting to do. Far away in the deep ocean, something else has started. Huge waves build up and charge toward the shore at hundreds of miles an hour. They crash against the coast and destroy buildings and **communities.**

Quake data

- Every week, worldwide, there are two or three strong earthquakes. Luckily, most of these take place in unpopulated places or deep under the ocean.

- Earthquakes at sea can create waves up to 100 feet (30 meters) high. These do serious damage when they hit the coast.

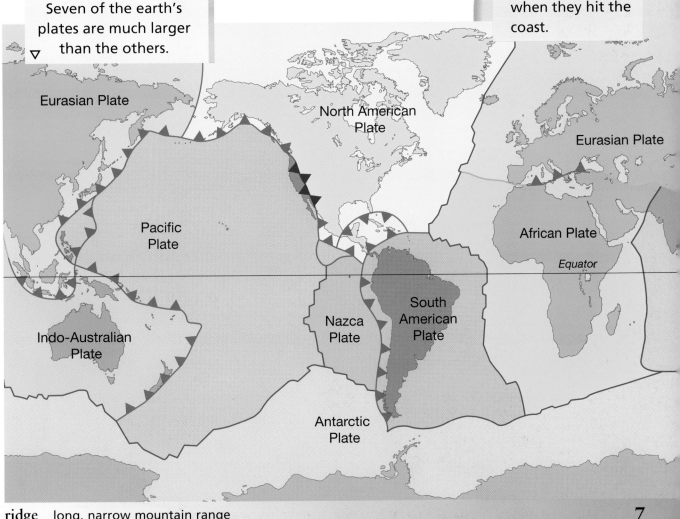

Seven of the earth's plates are much larger than the others. ▽

Eurasian Plate

North American Plate

Eurasian Plate

Pacific Plate

African Plate

Equator

Indo-Australian Plate

Nazca Plate

South American Plate

Antarctic Plate

ridge long, narrow mountain range
trench long, deep ditch in the ocean floor

Quake data

- The great San Francisco earthquake of 1906 told scientists a lot about how the plates of the earth's crust move against each other.

- The Appalachian Mountains were made by two plates moving toward each other in a **collision zone.**

Things that go bump

The **plates** that make up the earth's **crust** are all different shapes and sizes. They fit together almost like a jigsaw puzzle, but they are not a perfect fit. The plates are constantly bumping into each other and causing all sorts of things to happen.

The Great Rift Valley

Some plates have land on them. Some have ocean or sea on them. Part of the great African plate is slowly splitting off from the rest. This is causing a **rift,** or break, in the **continent.** Where this is happening, a **valley** is being made. This is called the Great Rift Valley.

Great mountain ranges like △ the Himalayas were formed by plate movement.

fault   line of weakness where one plate meets another
rift   breaking apart, separation

Faults

In between the massive plates of the earth's crust are splits, or **faults**. The plates move several inches each year, but this movement is not a smooth operation. Some faults slip down, while others are **thrust** up. Other plates slide along without moving up or down.

Flat earth?

As two plates move toward or away from each other, they can cause an earthquake. When the plates move apart, they make space for hot melted rock, called **magma**, to push up from deep within the earth. When it cools, magma becomes new rock on the earth's surface. Because of this, plates that move this way create a **constructive plate margin**—as the plates move apart, new crust is made, or constructed.

Ocean ridge

The continent of Africa sits on its own plate, as does South America. These two giant plates are moving apart at about 2 inches (5 centimeters) every year. This means that the Atlantic Ocean is slowly getting bigger. In the middle of the ocean there is a huge **trench** and a **ridge**. This is called the Mid-Atlantic Ridge.

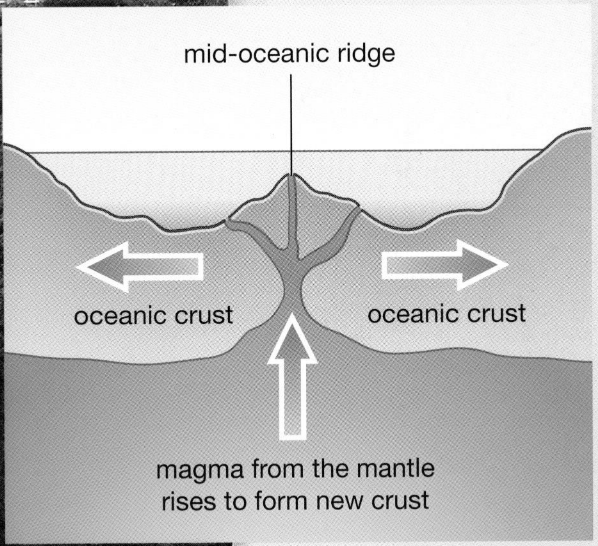

mid-oceanic ridge

oceanic crust

oceanic crust

magma from the mantle rises to form new crust

△ This diagram shows how the Mid-Atlantic Ridge formed.

◁ Africa's Great Rift Valley is almost 3,600 miles (6,000 kilometers) long. It has walls up to 1.2 miles (2 kilometers) high. Lakes are found on the valley floor.

thrust   push strongly

Sinking feeling

If an ocean **plate** moves toward a land plate, the ocean plate sinks beneath the land plate and is destroyed. This is because oceanic plate is heavier than the **continental** plate. This is called a **destructive plate margin** because something is broken.

Sudden movement

The sudden movement deep in the earth causes **shockwaves** that are sent out in all directions. When the shockwaves move upward, they cause a lot of damage to the earth's surface. If the center of the earthquake is below a town or city, the effects can be **devastating**. This is what happened in Gujarat, India, in 2001. The massive land plate that carries Europe and Asia moved toward the ocean plate that carries the Indian Ocean. The results were terrible.

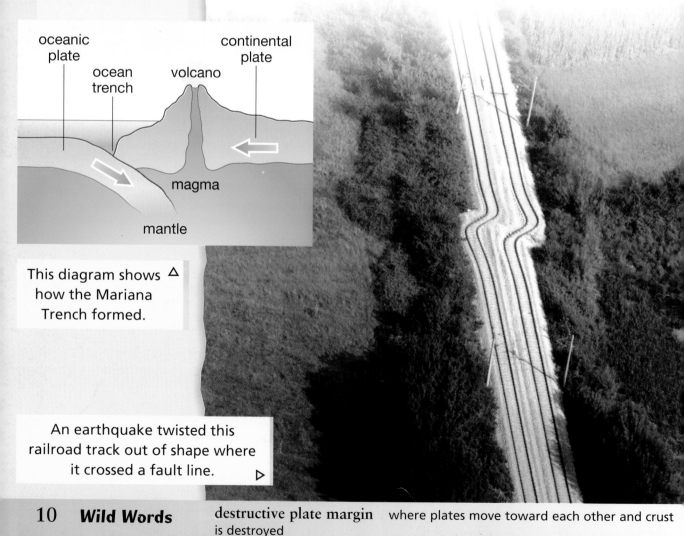

oceanic plate

ocean trench

volcano

continental plate

magma

mantle

This diagram shows △ how the Mariana Trench formed.

An earthquake twisted this railroad track out of shape where it crossed a fault line. ▷

destructive plate margin   where plates move toward each other and crust is destroyed

Fault lines

Very often, a **fault** line will appear on the surface of the earth without harming anybody. A fault is a line of weakness where one plate meets another. There are a lot of small plates of **crust,** so there are many fault lines all over the world. Sometimes, the fault line will appear suddenly. A road may unexpectedly **buckle** and crack because of crust slippage. Train tracks can bend. A neat line of trees can become crooked. Houses can slump, or slip down. And tall buildings? They can come tumbling down, crushing anyone and anything in their path. New fault lines occur because of **plate tectonics.** As the large plates move against each other, new lines of weakness are made.

Quake data

- An earthquake hit Gujarat on January 26, 2001.

- The Gujarat earthquake killed over 20,000 people.

- The worst damage was in a town called Bhuj.

Residents leaving Bhuj after the 2001 earthquake. ▽

Shockwaves

When two **plates** move together or try to slide past each other, **tension** builds up. These mighty pieces of rock are very strong. They can push against each other for years with neither side giving way. This is what is happening in California. The North American plate and the Pacific plate are trying to slide past each other. This is called a **conservative plate margin** because no **crust** is made or destroyed. The surface of the earth is kept stable.

The plates do not slide past each other smoothly. Rock has a lot of rough edges. Plates grind past each other and sometimes they stick. The pressure builds up and, eventually, they suddenly slip. This jerky movement causes earthquakes.

A **fault** line crack in the earth can be seen clearly in Red Canyon, Montana. ▽

Global Positioning System (GPS)   system of satellites that can figure out something's exact position on the earth

Harmless quakes?

The world's plates are moving all the time. It is a natural process, and you cannot even feel most earthquakes. But there is a big difference between an earthquake that causes no harm and one that destroys homes and lives. And when an earthquake is strong, it will leave you shaking.

Technology and tectonics

Scientists use all sorts of technology to measure the earth's movements. **Seismographs** produce records of earthquakes. These show how much the ground has moved and where the shaking was strongest. The **Global Positioning System (GPS)** uses satellites to pinpoint plate movement. This gives a precise measurement. Creepmeters are underground machines that measure how much the earth's plates shift, or creep.

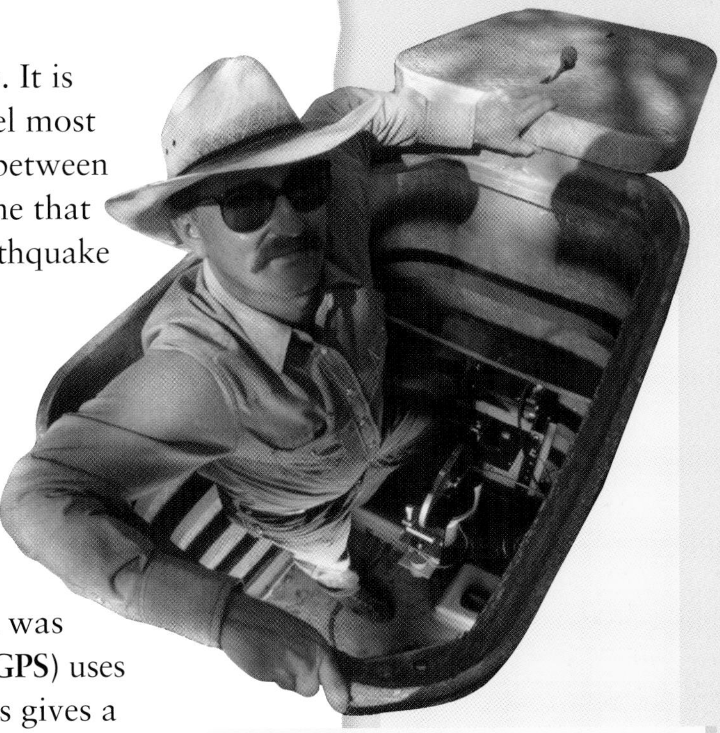

△ This man is checking an underground creepmeter. It can detect tiny ground movements, which might be the first signs of an earthquake.

Did you know . . . ?
The Gujarat earthquake of 2001 was felt thousands of miles away in Edinburgh, Scotland. Seismographs detected **shockwaves** ten minutes after the earthquake happened.

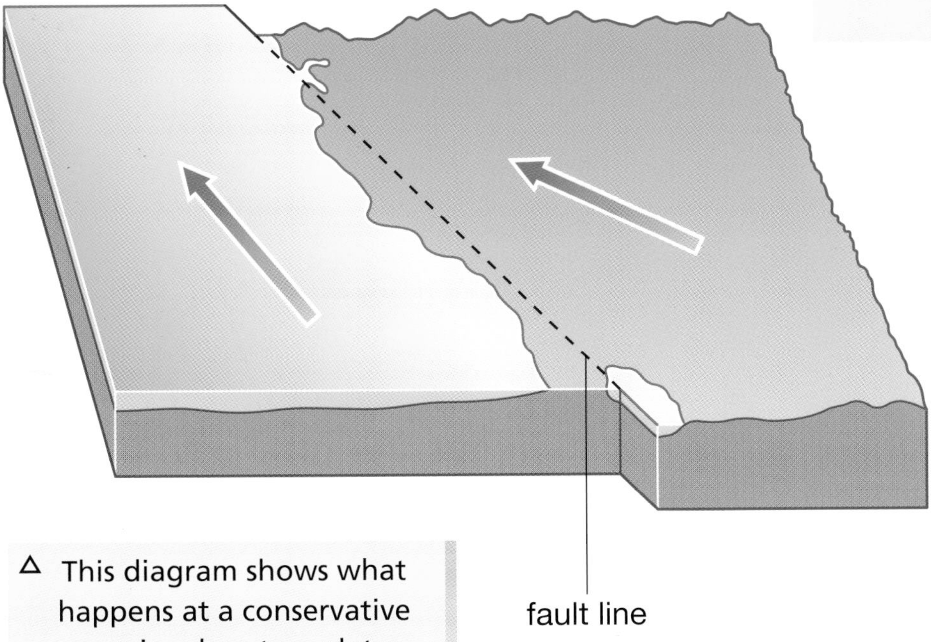

△ This diagram shows what happens at a conservative margin when two plates grind past one another.

fault line

seismograph   machine that measures earthquakes
tension   pressure

Shake, Rattle, and Roll

Earthquakes happen all the time. Most of them are not reported because they are too small for us to notice. Scientists monitor them to understand more about our planet. The most powerful earthquakes happen in an area known as the "Ring of Fire."

The Ring of Fire is an active earthquake zone. This means that large, destructive earthquakes usually happen in this area. The ring starts at Antarctica, circles the edges of the Pacific Ocean, and then runs down the length of North and South America. It is also where the most active volcanoes are found. The volcanoes here could erupt at any time.

△ The San Andreas strike-slip fault caused the Northridge earthquake of 1994. Roads and bridges across California were destroyed.

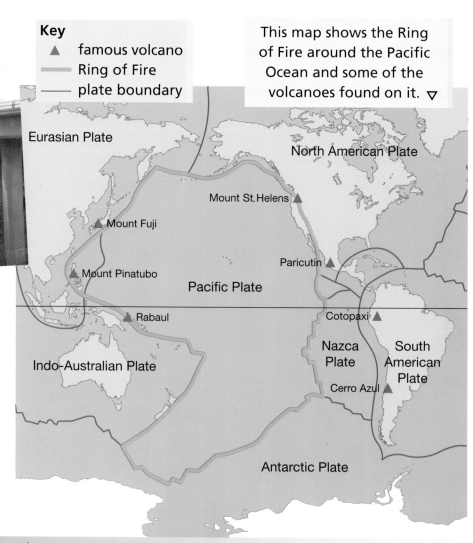

Key
- ▲ famous volcano
- ▬ Ring of Fire
- ── plate boundary

This map shows the Ring of Fire around the Pacific Ocean and some of the volcanoes found on it. ▽

Eurasian Plate

North American Plate

Mount St. Helens ▲

▲ Mount Fuji

Paricutin ▲

▲ Mount Pinatubo

Pacific Plate

Rabaul

Cotopaxi ▲

Nazca Plate

South American Plate

Indo-Australian Plate

Cerro Azul ▲

Antarctic Plate

active   alive, working
friction   force when two things rub together

Strike-slip faults

Probably the most famous earthquake zone on the earth is in California. Parts of California, including the cities of Los Angeles and San Francisco, lie between the massive Pacific plate and the North American plate. The **fault** in California is called the San Andreas Fault.

The San Andreas Fault has caused a lot of damage. It is a **strike-slip fault.** As the plates move, the **friction** created when they rub together causes them to stick and jam. When these sticking rocks break apart, they do so with such an explosive force that they produce earthquakes. Sometimes, they can cause new faults in the earth's crust. Strike-slip faults are also called **transform faults.**

Fault facts

- The San Andreas Fault is over 620 miles (1,000 km) long and 9 to 12 miles (15 to 20 km) deep.

- Each week, about 200 small quakes are measured along it.

△ The San Andreas Fault in California causes many earthquakes.

strike-slip fault   fault in which two plates try to push past each other and stick, eventually giving way with a sudden slip

Early machines used to record earthquakes in China used dragonheads and balls. When the ball fell out of the dragon's mouth, it meant the ground was about to shake. Today there are many ways to measure earthquakes, including the type of map below.

Other earthquake zones

Earthquakes out at sea mostly go unnoticed. Only the big quakes at sea cause large waves that can damage the coast. It is the earthquakes on land that are most dangerous to humans. And sometimes they happen in places you do not expect.

The English Midlands on the move

In 2002 two earthquakes were felt by people in the British cities of Manchester and Birmingham. Manchester was struck by 50 small earthquakes and **aftershocks.** Scientists are not sure why this happened. England is not near the edge of a **plate** where destructive earthquakes happen, as California is. So why Manchester? Maybe the earthquakes were caused by **shockwaves** that traveled through a weak line of rock in a plate. The source of the Manchester **tremors** was probably many hundreds of miles away.

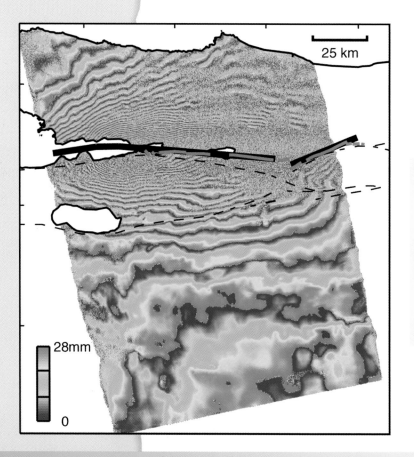

25 km

28mm

0

◁ This image was made using satellite pictures before and after an earthquake. It shows changes in the earth's surface. The closer the lines, the more the ground moved in that place.

aftershock   small tremor that follows a larger earthquake
intruder   someone who enters a place uninvited

Shaken awake

Here, two people tell their stories of the quakes in Britain.

Alan Odeku was fast asleep at home in Leicester when he was shaken awake by a terrifying tremor. At first he did not know what was happening. Then he realized that it was an earthquake. "The **shudders** went on for about ten or fifteen seconds, but it felt like it was much longer. The dresser moved across the bedroom floor and a lamp fell off the table."

In Leeds, Jackie Bream was affected by the Manchester quake. A shocking sound awoke her. "I thought there was an **intruder** in the house. But it was the dresser doors banging. It was frightening. I didn't think it could be an earthquake."

Seismology

Seismology is the study of earthquakes. A **seismologist** is a scientist who measures the tiniest movements in the earth's **crust**. Seismologists measure an earthquake and tell us how strong and how large it was.

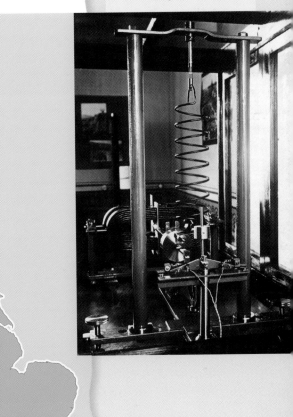

◁ This map shows the British cities that felt tremors in 2002.

SCOTLAND

Edinburgh

Leeds
Manchester
Liverpool
Leicester
WALES   Birmingham

ENGLAND

Cardiff
Bristol   London

seismologist   scientist who studies earthquakes
tremor   slight earthquake

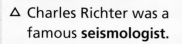

△ Charles Richter was a famous **seismologist**.

Thunder in the ground

There are not many warnings that earthquakes are going to happen. This makes them one of the greatest natural **hazards** of our planet. A series of little shakes, or **foreshocks,** will most commonly be the sign of bigger things to come. Just as there are distant rumblings of thunder in the sky during a storm, the ground rumbles during an earthquake.

Strange signs

People once used natural signs to **predict** earthquakes. Before an earthquake, ponds get smellier than usual. Underground, pressure is building up and gases leak into pond water. Some of these gases smell really bad. The temperature of ground water also changes. It becomes warmer and can also become cloudy. Animals can become jumpy just before a quake. It is as if they know what is going to happen—although this is not a very scientific sign.

Only the chimneys of some buildings were left standing after the San Francisco ▽ earthquake of 1906.

epicenter   point at which an earthquake reaches the earth's surface
foreshock   small tremor before the main earthquake

The measuring men

When we describe earthquakes, we talk about **magnitude.** This tells us the size and power of the shaking. There are two different ways to measure earthquake magnitude. Charles Richter invented the Richter Scale in the 1930s. This scale uses the strength of **vibrations** to figure out how powerful an earthquake is. It can be measured from anywhere on the earth, if we know the distance to the **epicenter.**

Giuseppe Mercalli invented the Mercalli Index in 1902. This figures out the strength of an earthquake in a particular area by describing how much shaking people can actually feel. Mercalli's original scale has been adapted and is known as the Modified Mercalli Index (MMI). An earthquake only has one Richter magnitude, but it can have many different Mercalli magnitudes. This is because a person standing close to the epicenter will feel vibrations more strongly than a person standing far away.

Giuseppe Mercalli factfile

- Born May 21, 1850, in Italy.

- Invented the Mercalli Index. This measures the force of an earthquake, from 1 to 12.

- This index describes earthquake damage that can be seen and felt.

- A 4-magnitude quake on the MMI means that windows rattle and walls crack. A 12-magnitude quake would cause massive destruction.

△This **seismograph** is from the Kobe earthquake of 1995. The quake measured 7.1 on the Richter Scale.

hazard   danger
magnitude   size and power of something

Shaken to the Core

Quake data

The tiny Japanese island of Okushiri was hit by a tsunami in 1993. The wave was almost 100 feet (30 meters) high and quickly swept ashore. The village on the island was flooded and destroyed within minutes.

When you throw a stone into a pond, it sends ripples across the surface. The same thing happens on a much bigger scale when the ground shakes.

Earthquakes can **trigger** all sorts of other events. They can cause landslides, floods, and fires and make volcanoes erupt. Most dangerous of all, they can set off big ripples across the surface of the ocean.

Terrifying tsunami

These ripples can create huge waves. The Japanese call them **tsunamis.** The waves can reach about 100 feet (30 meters) high. They get even taller and cause a lot of damage when they hit the land. Tsunamis can travel across the ocean at 500 to 600 miles (800 to 970 kilometers) per hour. There is nothing to stop this great force as it hits coastlines.

△ Tsunami **buoys** are put in the sea to measure wave patterns and give early warning of tsunamis.

△ The Hawaiian coast after a tsunami struck in 1960. Some houses were completely destroyed.

buoy   floating marker that may carry scientific instruments
trigger   be the cause of something

Mega-tsunami

Las Palmas in the Canary Islands is a volcanic island. One more large eruption could be enough to break off some of the island into the sea. If this happens, the tsunami could be 1,640 feet (500 meters) high. That is taller than the Empire State Building in New York. It would travel across the Atlantic Ocean within eight hours and hit New York, Boston, Miami, and many other communities. The results are **unthinkable.**

Italy, December 31, 2002

Stromboli eruption unleashes tsunami

A huge chunk of the island of Stromboli plunged into the sea after the island's volcano erupted yesterday. About 10 million cubic meters of rock and boiling lava slithered into the Mediterranean Sea, creating a tsunami that rocked ships over 100 miles (160 kilometers) away.

Tsunami waves are strong enough to flatten metal parking meters. ▽

tsunami   huge wave caused by a quake on the ocean floor or by a landslide
unthinkable   cannot be imagined

21

△ These apartments were destroyed in the Turkish quake of 1999.

The "big ones"

When a major earthquake happens, it is big news. These quakes are **devastating** natural disasters. After the ground shakes in these places, life is not the same again.

Magnitude with attitude: the Armenian earthquake

On December 7, 1988, a quiet country in the former **Soviet Union** was thrown into the spotlight. Many people had never heard of Armenia before then. But after that day, few would ever forget it.

The Armenian quake was so powerful that it went off the scale in all the world's **seismic** stations. It was too powerful to measure. The force of the **shockwaves** coming from 12 miles (20 kilometers) underground was compared to 100 nuclear bombs exploding. The entire landscape was changed and lives were altered forever— all in a few very scary seconds.

meteorite   lump of metal or rock from space
seismic   having to do with earthquakes

Flattened cities

The force of this earthquake was so great that it made huge cracks in rock, going several feet deep into the earth. Communication with the outside world was lost when lines and cables were ripped apart. Steel rails were twisted for miles and railroad embankments crumbled. Pipelines burst, leaking a **toxic** mixture of gas and oil. Steel towers fell down, and whole buildings were swallowed into the earth along with their **residents.** Four cities and towns were flattened like dominoes and turned into instant graveyards. By the time help arrived, it was too late to do anything other than pick up the pieces of a broken **community.** The number of dead was estimated at 25,000.

Big shakes

- In 1976 a quake in Tangshan, China, killed 250,000 people. The earthquake measured 8.2-**magnitude** on the Richter Scale.

- In the same year, an earthquake in Guatemala killed 23,000 people. It was 7.9-magnitude on the Richter Scale.

- An earthquake on the moon is called a moonquake.

△ This Armenian woman lost her home to the earthquake of 1988. Shockwaves from this quake traveled around the world for several days.

△ When space rocks called **meteorites** crash into the moon, they make the ground shake.

Soviet Union   group of countries once governed by Russia
toxic   poisonous

Quake data

The Kobe–Osaka raised highway in Japan was specially designed to wobble but not fall over in an earthquake. But the earthquake in 1995 was a 7.2-**magnitude** quake. It made 0.4 miles (600 meters) of the special highway topple sideways.

Kobe, 1995

Until January 17, 1995, Kobe was just another Japanese city. But more than 6,000 people were killed when an earthquake struck. Here is one person's **account** of what happened.

Stephani's story

"I was fast asleep in bed. Suddenly, my whole body went flying upward. As I landed, heavy things fell on top of me. I thought I was being attacked. Everything was smashing up and down all over the room. I felt total fear.

"It was completely dark. There was no power. I could hear glass smashing. I could also hear a huge deep grinding noise. I kept thinking 'I must get out.' I got out from under the furniture and I leaped toward the door."

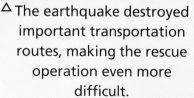

△ The earthquake destroyed important transportation routes, making the rescue operation even more difficult.

account   story of what happened
aftermath   time after a disaster

"Get out! Get out"

"I did not know what was happening. Was it an explosion or a bomb? I could not see, but I felt my way through and ran out of my apartment. The noise was really loud. I huddled under the **stairwell** at the bottom of the stairs with my neighbor. Then it stopped. All that happened in less than 45 seconds."

Aftermath

"After the shaking stopped, I ran down the street and helped people who were climbing out of the rubble. Lots of people were injured. There was no electricity or water.

"When I went back into my apartment, I could not believe what I saw. There was broken glass everywhere. I had jumped over a huge pile of glass with bare feet and not gotten a scratch."

Hard to believe

100,000 buildings were destroyed in the Kobe earthquake. More than 300,000 people were made homeless.

△ Water and gas pipes are cracked by big earthquakes, causing fires and floods.

◁ Most of the buildings in the **residential** area of Nagata were **devastated**. The quake started huge fires that destroyed almost 7,000 wooden buildings.

stairwell   space under a staircase

Northridge, California, 1994

Earthquakes in cities are the most destructive in terms of damage to people and places. The cost of rebuilding fallen buildings, transportation networks, and lost business can run into millions of dollars.

At 4:31 A.M. on January 17, 1994, the town of Northridge suffered a powerful earthquake. For fifteen terrifying seconds, the ground shook hard and changed a **community** forever. Ten highway bridges collapsed, railroads **buckled,** and buildings toppled. It was **chaos.** Because transportation was badly disrupted, the emergency services found it very hard to get to survivors. The final **toll** was 57 dead, 11,000 injured, and 20,000 homeless. But it could have been much worse.

△ An engraving of the Lisbon earthquake of 1755.

When a highway ▷ collapses, it is even more difficult to send out rescue teams.

avalanche   huge amount of snow and ice falling quickly down a mountain
chaos   confusion

Good Friday quake: Alaska, 1964

It was not a good Friday when this earthquake struck. Unlucky Alaska has had more earthquakes than any other U.S. state. The Good Friday quake lasted a massive four minutes and destroyed the city of Anchorage. Landslides and **avalanches** were set off, causing widespread **devastation**. The earthquake measured 9.2 on the Richter Scale.

Buildings rocked on their foundations, bridges buckled like cardboard, and houses snapped apart. If that was not enough, the quake also **triggered** a **tsunami** that crashed along the Alaskan coast. About 3,100 miles (5,000 kilometers) away, the ripple effect of tsunami waves reached and flooded the coast of Hawaii.

No resistance

Many houses and buildings collapsed in the Alaskan earthquake because they were made of wood. If they had been made of brick or another more **earthquake-resistant** material, they might not have crumbled so easily.

△ The Alaskan quake caused this whole street and a row of cars to drop 20 feet (6 meters) below normal level.

earthquake-resistant   able to survive an earthquake
lo(h   Scottish word for lake

Damage Limitation

On May 31, 1970, an earthquake dislodged ice in the Andes Mountains in Peru. The ice moved downhill, melting and mixing with the earth. It caused a huge mudslide that slid down the mountain at 200 miles (320 kilometers) per hour.

When the ground stops shaking, the problems caused by an earthquake have only just begun. The **aftereffects** can be far more **devastating.** More people die from drowning after earthquakes than from falling buildings during the quakes. This is because earthquakes often cause huge **tsunamis.** Very often, victims of the flood live thousands of miles away from where the earthquake took place. After the 1964 Good Friday earthquake in Alaska, Hawaii was devastated by a massive tsunami. The wave rocketed across the ocean and flooded the low-lying island.

Unlucky Lisbon, Portugal, 1755

In 1755 an earthquake far out in the Atlantic Ocean had a devastating effect on the city of Lisbon in Portugal. A quake more than 140 miles (300 kilometers) out at sea caused a huge tsunami that rolled toward the city. Buildings were destroyed and many thousands of people drowned.

△ The 1970 mudslide completely buried the town of Yungay. Almost 25,000 people were killed.

aftereffect   something that follows the main action

A frenzy of fire:
San Francisco, 1906

The San Francisco earthquake of 1906 is one of the worst disasters in the history of the United States. In 48 seconds the city changed forever. The quake caused gas pipes to burst. For three whole days, fires raged across the city. Many of the buildings were made of wood and burned quickly. Firefighters were helpless against such a mighty blaze. The sky was black with smoke, and thousands of people were made homeless.

The firestorms that followed the 1906 quake burned out of control for three days. They destroyed 30 schools, 80 churches, and 250,000 ▽ homes. Over 3,000 people were killed.

△ San Francisco's tallest building at the time was the Call skyscraper. It survived the quake but burned down in the fires that followed.

Factfile: Mount St. Helens

The **avalanche** moved at a speed of 80 miles (130 kilometers) per hour. Fifty-seven people died. Millions of trees were blown down. Almost 185 miles (300 kilometers) of roads were destroyed. Nearly 200 homes were ruined.

Rock and roll

Earthquakes can start floods and fires, but that is not all. When an earthquake hits a volcano, things are really going to get dangerous.

Mighty Mount St. Helens

The Cascade Mountains in the northwestern United States are visited by thousands of tourists each year. Previously, most people went to see Mount St. Helens, a beautiful snow-capped volcano. But on May 18, 1980, all visits were **abruptly** stopped by an unexpected event.

Early in the morning, about 0.9 miles (1.5 kilometers) beneath the volcano, an earthquake struck. This **triggered** one of the most powerful volcanic eruptions of the 20th century. Within a minute of the earthquake, Mount St. Helens rocked into life. A gigantic blast was followed by a massive eruption of **lava** fragments.

The landscape of Mount St. Helens would never be the same again. ▽

The eruption flattened trees, △ **polluted** lakes, and blasted a huge crater in the mountainside.

abruptly   suddenly
geologist   someone who studies rocks

Within two weeks, the ash from the eruption had traveled around the world. **Geologists** were shocked at both the suddenness and the power of the eruption. Even now, the landscape of the area has not returned to its former beauty. Some plants and flowers have poked through the ashy soil, but the landscape has been changed forever.

October 30, 2002

TERROR AS NEW QUAKE ROCKS ETNA

An earthquake rocked the Italian island of Sicily yesterday, sending streams of lava and ash from the volcano Mount Etna. The quake measured 4.4 on the Richter Scale. Hundreds of homes, shops, and a church were damaged in the main town.

△ Ten years after the eruption, the land around Mount St. Helens was still covered in ash and dead trees.

An earthquake ▷ caused a volcano to erupt in Italy in 2002.

lava   hot melted rock from a volcano
pollute   add harmful substances to air, water, or land

Quake data

- In 1959 an earthquake in Montana caused a highway to slump into a lake.

- The earthquake was 7.3-**magnitude** on the Richter Scale.

- Twenty-eight people died.

Bedrock

Depending on where you are in the world, earthquakes will do different amounts of damage. This depends on what type of rock surrounds you. Some rocks are soft and some are hard. **Bedrock** is the hardest rock of all. It is very hard to break. If your house is built on bedrock, it will probably survive an earthquake. But if it is built on softer rock, it will probably fall down during an earthquake. And if your house is built on soft wet soil, it might just start sinking.

△ Only small sections of this highway survived the 1959 earthquake in Montana.

bedrock   hardest rock of all
liquefaction   sand or soil that is heated until it becomes like liquid

Sinking soil

Liquefaction happens when the ground gets so hot or crumbly that it becomes **pulpy**, almost like a liquid. Anything that is built on ground that becomes liquefied will sink into it. The liquefied soil may also travel like a **mudflow** and bury whatever is in its path.

Liquefaction was a big problem in the Armenian and Indian earthquakes. Many houses were built on soft, sandy ground. When the earthquakes struck, the ground just gave way and the heat from below made it soft, like liquid. The buildings simply sank into the ground. When this has happened, it is very hard to repair the buildings afterward. Usually, they have to be built all over again, in a different **location.**

Quake shatters church of St. Francis

In 1997 the Italian hill town of Assisi was hit by a series of earthquakes. Part of the church of St. Francis was damaged when some of the roof fell in. Some famous wall paintings in the church were harmed by the shaking.

△ Older buildings are often the worst hit by earthquakes. Sadly, they can never be replaced.

◁ Roads seem to crack or crumble especially easily.

location   place
pulpy   very soft

Bingol, 2003

More than 100 people were killed and a thousand injured when a strong earthquake shook Turkey in May 2003. A school dormitory in the town of Bingol collapsed, trapping almost 200 sleeping students inside. Soldiers and rescuers dug through concrete slabs and tangled steel to try to save as many children as they could.

Search and rescue

After an earthquake, it is a race against time to find survivors. Rescue teams use special heat cameras and **rescue dogs** to help them find people trapped in fallen buildings. Power supplies are often **down** after a quake and roads may have collapsed, so it is hard for ambulances to get to the disaster site. Telephones may not work and computers might go offline.

Rescue dogs

Rescue teams use highly trained dogs to sniff out survivors. Different breeds of dogs are used, although they must be intelligent animals. They must also be in excellent physical condition. The dogs smell something belonging to missing persons and then use the scent to track them down.

A rescue dog hunts for survivors.

▽

Italian search and rescue teams scouring rubble using infrared cameras, blow torches, and their bare hands. ▷

down   out of action
floodlights   large, powerful lights used to light up areas at night

San Giulano di Puglia

When an earthquake struck Italy in 2002, the United Nations and the Red Cross assisted Italian rescue workers. Specialist equipment, such as **infrared cameras,** was used to help locate people buried under fallen buildings. For a few days, the small village of San Giuliano di Puglia became a **focus** for the world as rescuers struggled to find survivors.

RACE TO SAVE LIVES AS QUAKE KILLS CHILDREN

Italy, November 1, 2002

A school roof fell in and buried 30 children alive following an earthquake in a small Italian village. Rescue workers searched through the rubble last night with their bare hands. The race to rescue the children went on through the night under **floodlights.**

Ten-day quake ordeal

Ten days after an earthquake that **devastated** the Indian state of Gujarat, two survivors were pulled out of the rubble.

"
It was a delicate operation. If we had used bulldozers they would have been killed.
"

Rescue worker, Gujarat.

Rescue teams are trained to use helicopter lifts. ▷

focus   center of interest or activity
rescue dogs   dogs trained to find survivors by smell

A Crash Course in Survival

Sometimes, there are lucky escapes from earthquakes . . .

Trembling teacups!

In August 1996 Richard Hatherall was sitting in his office on the 41st floor of a **high-rise** in Tokyo, Japan. Suddenly, the building started rolling from side to side. "It wasn't a strong quake, but the table moved and my cup of tea spilled. It felt like I was on a boat. It certainly gave me the shakes!"

L.A. jolted awake

In October 1999 a 7-**magnitude** earthquake struck California. The **epicenter** was in the desert, away from houses. A train was **derailed** and power lines were brought down. Amazingly, no one was killed, even though millions of people in Los Angeles were awakened by the jolt.

△ This woman sleeps in an earthquake-proof bed with a roof!

available   within your reach
derailed   forced to leave the rails, or train tracks

Six steps to survival

1 If you are inside when the shaking starts, take shelter under a table to avoid being hit on the head by falling objects. If you are outdoors, find a clear spot away from buildings, trees, and power lines. Drop to the ground and cover yourself with anything available.

****

2 Stay still until the shaking stops and you are sure it is safe to exit. Stay away from windows.

****

3 After the shaking stops, check for injuries. Protect yourself from further danger by putting on long pants, a long-sleeved shirt, sturdy shoes, and gloves.

****

4 Look for fires and put them out. If you smell gas leaking, turn it off or get out.

****

5 Listen to the radio for instructions.

****

6 Expect aftershocks. Each time you feel one: Drop, cover, and hold on!

Packed for survival

Many companies in the United States give their workers earthquake survival packs. These contain useful survival objects such as a flashlight, matches, a cloth mask, and even playing cards!

Items in a typical earthquake survival pack. ▽

high-rise   building with many stories

Facing disaster

Many people across the world live in earthquake zones. They have learned to live with the daily threat of the earth shaking under them. Taking sensible **precautions** can reduce the risk of damage and harm. For example, in the United States, households are sent an earthquake-awareness leaflet. This tells people how to protect themselves and their homes during a serious quake.

Disaster Day

Every year on September 1, there is a Disaster Prevention Day **drill** in Japan. Millions of people practice emergency procedures in case of a volcanic eruption or an earthquake. Police, fire, and army workers practice what they will do if disaster strikes. Japanese people carry dust masks and hard hats. They practice getting to special evacuation centers quickly. Even pets are trained to behave themselves!

△ Leyla, a 3-year old girl, is rescued from her school dormitory, where she was trapped by the Bingol earthquake in Turkey in May 2003.

Children in Kagoshima, Japan, wearing their protective hats. ▽

Be prepared

People who live in earthquake **hotspots** need to be ready. Storing spare food, bottled water, a radio, a flashlight, and a first-aid kit is a good idea. A whistle is useful for attracting the attention of rescuers.

drill   practice
engineer   person who designs and builds things

Neighborhood watch

Another way people organize themselves is by joining together as a **community**. In some places, there are City Emergency Preparedness committees. These are made up of people from neighborhood groups, firefighters, Red Cross workers, and police. The different groups come together to plan how they will manage an earthquake emergency.

Global village

When a major earthquake like the one in Gujarat or Armenia strikes, countries around the world offer help. The United Nations, the Red Cross, and the World Food Program are quick to respond. In addition to sending doctors, **engineers**, helicopters, and rescue equipment, they also supply things such as blankets, medicine, and tents to help ease the crisis.

Information leaflets about earthquake safety can be found on the Internet. ▷

Earthquake — USGS — American Red Cross

Are You Ready for an Earthquake?
Here's what you can do to prepare for such an emergency

Prepare a Home Earthquake Plan

✓ Choose a safe place in every room—under a sturdy table or desk or against an inside wall where nothing can fall on you.

✓ Practice DROP, COVER, AND HOLD ON at least twice a year. Drop under a sturdy desk or table, hold on, and protect your eyes by pressing your face against your arm. If there's no table or desk nearby, sit on the floor against an interior wall away from windows, bookcases, or tall furniture that could fall on you. Teach children to DROP, COVER, AND HOLD ON!

✓ Choose an out-of-town family contact.

✓ Consult a professional to find out additional ways you can protect your home, such as bolting the house to its foundation and other structural mitigation techniques.

✓ Take a first aid class from your local Red Cross chapter. Keep your training current.

✓ Get training in how to use a fire extinguisher from your local fire department.

✓ Inform babysitters and caregivers of your plan.

Eliminate hazards, by—

✓ Bolting bookcases, china cabinets, and other tall furniture to wall studs.

✓ Installing strong latches on cupboards.

✓ Strapping the water heater to wall studs.

Prepare a Disaster Supplies Kit for home and car, including—

✓ First aid kit and essential medications.

✓ Canned food and can opener.

✓ At least three gallons of water per person.

✓ Protective clothing, rainwear, and bedding or sleeping bags.

✓ Battery-powered radio, flashlight, and extra batteries.

✓ Special items for infant, elderly, or disabled family members.

✓ Written instructions for how to turn off gas, electricity, and water if authorities advise you to do so. (Remember, you'll need a professional to turn natural gas service back on.)

✓ Keeping essentials, such as a flashlight and sturdy shoes, by your bedside.

Know what to do when the shaking begins

✓ DROP, COVER, AND HOLD ON! Move only a few steps to a nearby safe place. Stay indoors until the shaking stops and you're sure it's safe to exit. Stay away from windows. In a high-rise building, expect the fire alarms and sprinklers to go off during a quake.

✓ If you are in bed, hold on and stay there, protecting your head with a pillow.

✓ If you are outdoors, find a clear spot away from buildings, trees, and power lines. Drop to the ground.

✓ If you are in a car, slow down and drive to a clear place (as described above). Stay in the car until the shaking stops.

Identify what to do after the shaking stops

✓ Check yourself for injuries. Protect yourself from further danger by putting on long pants, a long-sleeved shirt, sturdy shoes, and work gloves.

✓ Check others for injuries. Give first aid for serious injuries.

✓ Look for and extinguish small fires. Eliminate fire hazards. Turn off the gas if you smell gas or think it's leaking. (Remember, only a professional should turn it back on.)

✓ Listen to the radio for instructions.

✓ Expect aftershocks. Each time you feel one, DROP, COVER, AND HOLD ON!

✓ Inspect your home for damage. Get everyone out if your home is unsafe.

✓ Use the telephone only to report life-threatening emergencies.

Your local contact is:

hotspot   area that gets a lot of earthquakes
precaution   safety measure taken in advance

The Future

Still standing

Some of the most effective **earthquake-resistant** designs can be found in the most surprising places. Bamboo and wood are flexible materials. This means they will bend.

Today, **seismologists** have a lot of new technology to help them **predict** when an earthquake may strike and how powerful it might be. There are **seismic stations** all over the world. These are where **shockwaves** and **vibrations** are measured. Scientists also use the **Global Positioning System (GPS)** to figure out how far the earth's plates have moved. This is so accurate, they can tell within a few inches where the **epicenter** of a quake is.

The Transamerica Pyramid in San Francisco has been designed to stand up ▽ to strong earthquakes.

△ Huts made from bamboo and wood in the Andes in South America stay standing even after massive earthquakes.

pagoda   Hindu or Buddhist religious building with a layered tower
rigid   stiff, cannot bend

Reducing risk

Maps that show where shaking will be worst or where buildings are weakest help governments and emergency services to plan for a quake. They educate local people about what to do if an earthquake strikes.

California is probably better prepared for earthquakes than anywhere else in the world. This is why, despite severe earthquakes, the number of deaths there is usually quite low.

Pagodas such as the Kofukuji▷ Temple in Japan have always stood up to earthquakes. We can learn from their design.

Thinking ahead

California has strict building laws. All new buildings are built to cope with quakes. They are designed to shake. Building across a **fault** line is forbidden because, if the ground shook, the building would be torn apart. Scientists and **engineers** can improve the design of buildings by studying how structures behave in a quake.

A model future?

Engineers in Japan, the United States, and other earthquake **hotspots** around the world are finding new ways to make buildings safer. Some new **high-rises** are now being built on rollers so that the whole structure can move when the ground shakes. Because the buildings are not **rigid,** it means they do not resist the power of the earthquake. Some buildings are built on tough rubber springs to allow them to sway.

Quake data

- On February 29, 1960, a huge earthquake rocked the old town of Agadir in Morocco. Ten thousand people were killed by falling stone.

- In 1,400 years, only two pagodas have collapsed from quakes.

seismic station   remote place where earthquakes are measured by machines

Tectonic plates move apart in Djibouti, causing huge cracks in the landscape. ▽

Earthwatch

Despite the help of technology, it is very hard to **predict** when the next big earthquake will strike. But scientists can see which parts of the world are very active by looking at past earthquakes. They believe that there is an 80 percent chance that the northwestern part of the United States will be the victim of a major earthquake within the next twenty years. And of course, there is always the San Andreas Fault near San Francisco to monitor.

Countries such as the United States and Japan have "disaster plans" in case of earthquakes. The plans are put together by scientists, city planners, **engineers**, and rescue **personnel**. These plans explain what the police, army, firefighters, and hospitals will do if the ground starts to shake. Other than that, it is a question of waiting.

Dramatic landscape

The earth is moving all the time. In some places, such as Djibouti, Africa, you can see the powerful forces at work right in front of your eyes. The plate movements and volcanic eruptions in Djibouti make it perfect for studying earthquakes.

personnel   workers
vibration   small, fast movements backward and forward

Turbulent planet

Because of **plate** movement, the surface of the earth will continue to alter. The grinding of the plates and pressure on the edges of plates will cause earthquakes. Earthquakes will bring volcanic eruptions and towering **tsunamis** along for the ride.

The earth trembles all the time without our even noticing. We are so used to cars and trucks thundering along the roads that a few extra minor **vibrations** from underground are easily ignored. It is only the really big ones that count. Earthquakes are always going to happen. It is not a question of if, but when.

That was a **bad** one. Things were bouncing.

Los Angeles **resident** Lucille Manning in 1999.

◁ In countries such as the U.S., buildings can be strengthened against future earthquakes. Here, an engineer is checking equipment underneath City Hall in Los Angeles.

Find Out More

Organizations

Earthquakes

The U.S. Geological Survey runs this site, which is full of information, quake updates, and links to other websites.

earthquake.usgs.gov

Seismological Lab

The University of Nevada's site offers illustrated lectures, one-page information sheets, a book listing, and other sources on earthquakes.

seismo.unr.edu

Books

Coster, Patience. *Disasters in Nature: Earthquakes*. Chicago: Heinemann Library, 2000.

Deedrick, Tami. *Nature on the Rampage: Earthquakes*. Chicago: Raintree, 2003.

Steele, Christy. *Nature on the Rampage: Tsunamis*. Chicago: Raintree, 2003.

World Wide Web

If you want to find out more about earthquakes, you can search the Internet using keywords such as these:

- earthquake + [country]
- "Global Positioning System"
- meteorite + earthquakes
- "destructive plate margin"
- seismologist
- "rescue dog" + earthquake
- mudflow
- "plate tectonics"

You can also find your own keywords by using headings or words from this book. Use the search tips below to help you find the most useful websites.

Search tips

There are billions of pages on the Internet, so it can be difficult to find exactly what you want to find. For example, if you just type in "water" on a search engine such as Google, you will get a list of 85 million web pages! These search skills will help you find useful websites more quickly:

- Know exactly what you want to find out about first.
- Use simple keywords instead of whole sentences.
- Use two to six keywords in a search, putting the most important words first.
- Be precise—only use names of people, places, or things.
- If you want to find words that go together, put quote marks around them—for example, "shield volcano" or "**pyroclastic flow.**"
- Use the advanced section of your search engine.
- Use the + sign to add certain words.

Where to search

Search engine

A search engine looks through the entire web and lists all the sites that match the words in the search box. It can give thousands of links, but the best matches are at the top of the list, on the first page. Try **google.com.**

Search directory

A search directory is more like a library of websites that have been sorted by a person instead of a computer. You can search by keyword or subject and browse through the different sites in the same way you would look through books on a library shelf. A good example is **yahooligans.com.**

Glossary

abruptly   suddenly

account   story of what happened

active   alive, working

aftereffect   something that follows the main action

aftermath   time after a disaster

aftershock   small tremor that follows a larger earthquake

available   within your reach

avalanche   huge amount of snow and ice falling quickly down a mountainside

bedrock   hardest rock of all

buckle   twist or bend out of shape

buoy   floating marker that may carry scientific instruments

chain reaction   when one thing causes another to happen

chaos   confusion

collision zone   area in which plates move together and crumple upward to form fold mountains

communities   places or towns where people live together

conservative plate margin   place at which plates try to slide past each other and no crust is formed or destroyed

constructive plate margin   place at which plates pull apart and new crust is formed

continent   one of the earth's seven large land masses

core   ultrahot center of the earth

crevice   narrow crack or opening in the earth or rock

crust   outer layer of rock around the earth on which the oceans and land sit

derailed   forced to leave the rails or tracks

destructive plate margin   place in which plates move toward each other and crust is destroyed

devastate   cause great destruction

down   out of action

drill   practice

earthquake-resistant   able to survive an earthquake

engineer   person who designs and builds things

epicenter   point at which an earthquake reaches the earth's surface

fault   line of weakness where one plate meets another

floodlights   large, powerful lights used to light up areas at night

focus   center of interest or activity

foreshock   small tremor before the main earthquake

friction   force when two things rub together

geologist   someone who studies rocks

Global Positioning System (GPS)   system of satellites that figure out something's exact position on the earth

hazard   danger

high-rise   building with many stories

hotspot   area that gets a lot of earthquakes

infrared camera   camera that detects heat instead of light, so it shows warm bodies

intruder   someone who enters a place uninvited

jolted   shaken suddenly

lava   hot, melted rock from a volcano

liquefaction   sand or soil that is heated and becomes like a liquid

location   place

loch   Scottish word for lake

magma   superhot liquid rock

magnitude   size and power of something

mantle   superhot rock and gas layer that surrounds the earth

megaquake   earthquake measuring 8 or more on the Richter Scale

meteorite   lump of metal or rock from space

mudflow   fast-flowing river of mud

pagoda   Hindu or Buddhist religious building with a layered tower

personnel   workers

plate tectonics   movements of the earth's plates

plate   one of the huge sections of rock that form the earth's crust

pollute   add harmful substances to air, water, or land

precaution   safety measure taken in advance

predict   say when something will happen

pulpy   very soft

rescue dog   dog trained to find survivors by smell

resident   person who lives in a certain place

ridge   long, narrow mountain range

rift   breaking apart, separation

rigid   stiff, cannot bend

seismic   having to do with earthquakes

seismic station   place where earthquakes are measured by machines

seismograph   machine that measures earthquakes

seismologist   scientist who studies quakes

shockwaves   forces that are created by an earthquake deep underground

shudder   hard shake

Soviet Union   group of countries once governed by Russia

stairwell   space under a staircase

strike-slip fault   fault in which two plates try to push past each other and stick, eventually giving way with a sudden slip

tension   pressure

thrust   push strongly

toll   amount of damage caused by a disaster

toxic   poisonous

transform fault   another name for a strike-slip fault

tremor   slight earthquake

trench   long, deep ditch in the ocean floor

trigger   cause something

tsunami   huge wave caused by an earthquake on the ocean floor or a landslide

unthinkable   cannot be imagined

valley   lower area of land between hills or mountains

vibration   small, fast movements backward and forward

Index